THE PATH TO

COURAGE

THE PATH TO

COURAGE

7 Steps to Follow Your Soul Song and Live Your Happily EPIC After

DEBBIE BURNS

Path to Courage
7 Steps to Follow Your Soul Song and Live Your Happily EPIC After

Author Photo courtesy of Meagan Smith
Formatting by D Tinker Editing

ISBN: 978-1-7321472-1-8

22 21 20 19 18   1 2 3 4 5

For the visionaries, creators, artists, writers, and sacred rebels who inspire me every day to choose courage over fear.

YOU are my why. And your stories are the answer to my Soul Song.

When you find the thing that sets your soul on fire, pursue it with everything you have, and be awed by what can happen when you choose to truly live.

CONTENTS

Do you have the courage?
Do you have the courage to bring forth this work?
The treasures that are hidden inside you are
hoping you will say yes.

~Jack Gilbert
(as quoted by Elizabeth Gilbert), *Big Magic*

Your journey begins here:
www.SacredRebels.me

LETTER IN A BOTTLE:

Dear Sacred Rebel

I HEAR YOUR SOUL SONG calling, that burning desire deep down in your gut (no, it's not indigestion) that says you are meant for something bigger, something greater, something . . . *more*.

Not to be an attention grabber, but a significance maker—creating meaning and impact in everything you do. You want your life to matter, to be bigger than just "this" (whatever "this" is right now). You want to live a life of joy and fulfillment, waking every morning with purpose and passion as you leave your footprints on the hearts of the people you serve.

And you want the thrill of feeling truly alive . . . *now*, in this moment. Not by jumping from planes (though that can totally be your thing), but by really *living* in a way that aligns with YOU, freed from the "shoulds" and "have-tos" of the talking heads of your past and maybe even your present.

You want adventure! Tasting life and experiencing new horizons. Whether that comes from fully savoring your own backyard or traveling across the globe to explore different cultures, you know that life has so much more to offer and you want to be part of it.

You want to *influence* it.

Do you feel that? The warmth spreading through your body, increasing the rhythm of your heart as you realize that—YES!—I am talking to *you*. I see you, I feel you. And I know both the power and the terror of allowing one's self to really entertain the possibility of the Big Dream—which is the shape our Soul Song takes as we reach out into the world. I've experienced that same pounding heartbeat, the same slightly shaking limbs, the same scratch at my throat. And I want you to know this isn't a pipe dream, but *your* dream—worth pursuing and worth living.

Magic happens when we sing our Soul Songs and, Friend, it's time for you to sing!

Loves & hugs,

Deb

INTRODUCTION:

Bring Me to Life

FOR THOSE WHO DON'T KNOW me and those who do, welcome, welcome, welcome to *The Path to Courage!*

fires glitter cannons

(I have got to get me a real-life set of those cannons because this kind of stuff—talking courage and big dreams—just makes me so freaking giddy!)

I love you, I love you, I love you. I am so grateful you are here. Thank you for choosing you and your Big Dream.

And great googley mooglies!!!! I am so crazy excited about what I have in store for you! But first and foremost, let's talk. You might be wondering, "Deb, what the dump is this? What is it all about? What am I getting myself into?" I want to be clear from the start . . . you're getting yourself into some kickass, amazing, deep-soul training. You need to know you deserve it. YOU are worth it. And so is this Soul Song singing from deep inside you.

This book is my invitation to you:

Come play with me! Come step into this world of courage and big dreaming and fulfilled living that feeds your soul and makes you feel alive. I want you to experience, as I do, the exhilarating joy of seeing your creations—in whatever form they take—move from dream to possibility to probability to inevitability.

End of story.

And I'm not going to make any bones about that. I'm not going to try and hide that from you. This is my opportunity to give you a taste of what life could look like, feel like, *be* like if you just had the courage to follow your dreams.

Because if you're here then you're already wondering, "What's the next step for me in my journey?" And it's imperative that we feed that curiosity with courage rather than fear.

No Hell Maybes

Let's make a deal, shall we?

When your soul shouts HELL YES, you jump on it. Whatever that is, okay? We spend way too much time doubting our intuition, doubling back when our soul says GO! We end up unhappy and unfilled. I've learned that when the soul says YES, you take the step—like Indiana Jones (in *The Last Crusade*) avoiding the rotating saws in the Grail Temple. The whisper came, a tiny indicator that he needed to move, and he dove forward. (Don't be like the other guys who got their heads chopped off. They didn't listen to the whisper.) You can pause to make sure you're jumping to the next platform and not off a cliff, but don't turn back. Don't wait for it to all make sense up there in your noggin. Don't double back afterward because Fear got you to change your mind.

If it's a HELL YES, do it. Do it now. And *trust* that your soul, God, and the Universe have your back.

Now, if your soul says HELL NO, you stop. None of this, "But Deb! I really want XYZ!" Nope. Do not do it. Don't let your brain think it knows better than your soul. It doesn't. It's an excellent companion to the soul, but it doesn't know everything and can't see all the facts. Our soul operates on a different plane and, whether we know it or not, it sees and experiences things our logical self doesn't. So please trust it when it shouts, like the big stone faces in *Labyrinth,* "This is not the way!"

HELL NO (or NOT RIGHT NOW) is perfectly okay. Whatever version of NO you receive, you don't owe anyone (including me!) an excuse or explanation.

And . . . if you're a HELL MAYBE . . . stop it! Get off the fence. Maybe keeps us stuck, like a pileup on the only freeway during rush hour. It's bad chicken and it doesn't just impact that one thing, it creates stuck-ness in *all* things in life because "maybe" is a "non-move." It's a holding tank of potential energy that can't be used to step forward because it's busy being used to hold space. Not intention or power . . . just empty space. Meaning all that energy that could be freed with a NO and then used to give a YES more power? You're keeping it all tied up in that one little word: MAYBE.

So, if you're feeling the HELL MAYBE, it's time to take a deeper look at the fear that is getting in your way of the YES/NO and move that bad boy out! (Don't worry, I'll show you exactly how to do that later. I got you boo!)

In the meantime, be committed to really leaning into what your intuitive soul is telling you. Be a HELL YES or a HELL NO with the caveat that you can always change your mind later. Just #nohellmaybes, okay?

Be in alignment with you. That's all I ask. (It's all anyone should ask.)

Your intuitive soul is worthy of your trust.

Got it? Awesome!

BEHIND THE GLITTER:

Deb on Soul Songs and Big Dreams

Q: What's the difference between a Soul Song and a Big Dream?

A: To me, a Soul Song is the inner call you feel to create meaning with your life, while the Big Dream is the *shape* that Soul Song takes.

For example, my Soul Song started nudging me to create greater meaning and impact in my life in my mid-twenties. It came in the form of feeling like there had to be *more* to this life than waking up, working my 9–5, coming home, eating, and going back to sleep only to repeat the cycle all over again. I knew I needed to do something different, I just didn't know what that was until my thirties. (Hard to hear your Soul Song when you're focused on meeting others' expectations.) When I finally listened, I realized my Soul Song was asking me to be a satellite dish, magnifying the message of higher love—a love that encompasses justice, mercy, gratitude, forgiveness, compassion, healthy boundaries and more—for self, others, and a Higher Power. But what shape would that take? *How* would I share this message and create impact in this way?

Enter the Big Dream. Once upon a time that looked like being a fiction writer—sharing truth through my stories. That's all I wanted. I didn't see anything more to it. So I followed that path. Over time it has morphed into confidence mentor, master intuitive, writing coach, integration guide, business strategist, and now—as you see me—a co-conspirator on your path to courage and authenticity. Never *losing* any of those pieces but *adding to* the treasure trove of experience and knowledge I've picked up along the way.

What I've learned is this: If you continue to say HELL YES when the Big Dream says, "This is next," the Big Dream keeps expanding . . . reaching more people and touching more lives.

I believe our Soul Songs and Big Dreams have seasons.

I am still in the season of "love" for my Soul Song. It's the undercurrent (the who and why) of everything I do and the decisions I make.

And I have experienced several different seasons of my Big Dream. It's the ship (the what and how) riding the undercurrent toward my newest destination. A ship that, for me, continues to get upgraded in shape, size, and speed as I continue to say HELL YES to my Big Dream.

For you, it could be different. It could be *one* Soul Song and *one* Big Dream. Or *one* Soul Song and *two* Big Dreams. It could even be a few Soul Songs (each a variant on that why) that still leads you toward that *one* Big Dream. Whatever the combination, it's about *you* finding *your* way. It's your path to walk and your discovery to make.

When you choose to follow that path, you become what I call a Sacred Rebel—a creator connected to a higher purpose, living outside the box and serving the world in a way only *you* can as you blaze a trail to your personal promised land.

Have a question? Send me your insights and comments. I want to know what you think!

https://www.debbieburns.me/contact

CHAPTER ONE:

You Are the One

YOU ARE THE ONE, the right one, the beautifully imperfect one who has been called to change the world.

And I've been looking for you.

Yes, *you.*

The visionary creator and sacred rebel sitting on the other side of these words with a whole big world starting to open up before you. A world of freedoms and possibilities and . . . fear. I hear your Soul Song and feel the power of your Big Dream. And when I look at this sacred creation that is trying to come into the world through you, I see not just your potential but your inevitability. *If* you lean in. *If* you say yes.

If you answer the call.

Because the truth is, I'm not here for everybody. I'm not here to work with or influence every human on the planet. I'm here to work with those visionary creators willing to wake up and shake up their true selves and create meaning and impact with their lives. *That's* who I'm looking for, because here's the belief I hold:

You have the power to change the world, but only if you choose it.

I want you to sit with that for a sec. Those tend to sound like very fluffy—probably very clichéd—nonsense words. "Ooo, I can change the world" (followed by an exaggerated eye roll). That's why I want you to sit with it for a moment. Let it sink in. Allow yourself to envision the possibilities . . . the "what ifs" that *could be* if you really did this big thing.

See it. Feel it. Hold it.

Because guess what, friend . . . our planet needs healing. Our nations and our humanity, they all need healing. And there is power IN YOU to do that—through your story, your experience, and your willingness to be vulnerable and show up and speak from your heart.

The *way* in which we impact the world will look different, but *the power to change* it—starting with our personal worlds, which spills over into our communities, our tribes and (if we want it) the entire world—that is the same. From Elaine Williams teaching people how to be in harmony with their bodies and Birdy Jones helping kids love who they are through her picture books to Malala Yousafzai standing up for women's rights to education and Tegla Loroupe advocating for peace, we all have an impact we can make.

That's why I get so passionate about this work! Because I *know* the power and importance you will play on the global scale. I *know* it. And it pains me deeply to see so much goodness locked away behind fear. So much greatness silenced by doubt, failure, and mental gremlins.

Together, you and I and the other visionaries on this planet are the tidal wave that can sweep away the negativity that has swarmed our people. But only if we, first, stand up for ourselves and, second, stand up for each other.

I stand for you!!! And I will stand up every single time to tell you that you matter, your story matters, and there *is* power in the words that come from your heart and in the passion spilling from your work. And for those sacred rebels who want to run toward their greatness? I am here to help them do it.

I believe that's you.

That's why you're holding this book, reading

its pages, leaning in to what I have to teach you. Because you want this . . . even *more* than I want this for you.

Who Am I? Oh, Yeah! Hi . . . I'm Deb!

Oh, my great jumpin' Jehoshaphat!!! I haven't even told you who I am yet. YIKES!!!! (I get so excited that I dive right in and forget to introduce myself all the time, lol.)

    face palm

    waves a hearty hello

I'm Deb, an ass-kicking Courage and Authenticity Coach who helps sacred rebels wake up and shake up their true selves to create meaning and impact with their lives. I'm talking about believing in yourself so strongly that the world can't help but believe in you too!

I'm a Molotov cocktail in Hello Kitty packaging who's been navigating trauma for the last 30+ years, weaving those truths into commercial fiction for the last 8, coaching visionary creators for the last 3, and firing glitter cannons since I realized I actually *do* like the color pink. I'm known to blend personal development principles with a little bit of woo (energy, intuitive gifts, chakras, auras, and all that jazz!) and a whole lotta love to help you build the courage to be seen on your journey of expression, personal freedom, leadership, and belonging. Your voice *needs* to be heard!

I've snorkeled the Palancar Reef and stood on the pyramids of Teotihuacan. I've crossed the Golden Gate Bridge and shed tears at the 9/11 Memorial. And I've traversed my own personal dark night of the soul (read: post-traumatic stress disorder) to come out the other side with a few scars, a deeper love of self, and an immovable commitment to live a life true to me.

And now I'm committed to helping you create that for yourself. (Not the scars part, the self-love and live-true-to-yourself part.)

Best part? You don't have to wait for someday.

Live Happily EPIC After . . . Right Now!

Every day I get to live my Soul Song!!! I get to sleep in—wahoo!!! (What? That's a big deal to me, #nojudging.) I get to have deep, meaningful conversations with fulfillment seekers and big dreamers, helping them embrace courage and achieve breakthroughs. I get to pursue my passions in writing. I get to speak on podcasts and stages, spreading this message that you *can* and you *will* and you *are* exactly the right person to do this Big Thing!!! I get to attend business retreats and conferences, meeting other amazing leaders all the time as we engage in both business dialogues and phenomenal, life-affirming conversations.

I get to experience a deep, deep connection with my spouse that has only grown more fulfilling as I've traveled this Soul Song road. I get to live reassured that I don't have to sacrifice relationships and connection to be a powerful woman leader. In fact! My relationships have *expanded* because of this journey—my tribe swelling to include the best mentors, coaches, peers, and clients a girl could ever ask for!

And, super important to me, I get to travel the world (last year I took 19 trips to 17 different cities) as I live my Happily EPIC After, creating meaning and impact in everything I do.

It's life *exactly* as I design it to be, with joy, fulfillment, adventure, and *feeling ALIVE* . . . all anchored by my own set of rules.

But It Hasn't Always Been this Way

It used to be a lot, LOT worse.

October 16, 2008:

I lay on the credit union floor, tummy down and fingers pressed against the rough industrial carpet as the gunman closed the door to our office. I was working as an assistant manager at the time— one more job in a long list of disappointments. I'd left my last administrative job to "put up my sails and see where the wind takes me" (actual words I used in my resignation letter), though working in a mom & pop credit union wasn't exactly what I'd had in mind. It kinda fell into my lap as a temporary job that accidentally turned into a permanent one.

Now, it seemed, as I listened to Mr. Bandana closing the door, that "Assistant Branch Manager" would be my final title.

I couldn't see him from the ground, but I imagined him locking the door, stepping back over to me, and putting a bullet into my head. Yet no scenes flashed before my eyes. I didn't even feel panic. (I blame shock.) Instead, as I lay there waiting to die, all I felt was a deep regret that I hadn't done more with my life.

I would die before I even had the chance to live.

And it was all my fault.

Not because I held the gun or had somehow summoned the Universe to drag a convicted felon on parole into my credit union (I think there is more to the "law of attraction" than 1+1=2), but because, out of all the chances I'd had to taste life—an all-expense-paid "road trip" to France, an Egyptian tour, two study abroad programs, a South

African excursion and more—, I'd turned them all down because I didn't have the time or the funds *or the courage* to take a risk.

Practical Deb had a path to follow—high school, college, career, marriage, house, kids—and I was still on baby step number two . . . "pay off debt."

"Pursue dreams" wasn't even on the list!

I'd followed all "their" rules. I'd crossed my t's and dotted my i's and had the house, the car, the job . . . but to what end? I wasn't happy. And now I would be dead.

Wasn't my life worth more than that? Wasn't I?

Not to ruin the ending, but I survived.

I fought and clawed and cried my way through post-traumatic stress disorder with all its accompanying friends: depression, anxiety, high suicidality and panic (yep, it finally hit me).

I even landed myself in a hospital because I didn't want to stay on this planet anymore. It was a terrifying, difficult decision filled with shame and remorse.

"I will never be the same after this," I thought. "And if people find out, they will never treat me the same either."

And can I just say, I am SO glad I turned out to be right on the first account and hella wrong on the second!!! Because I LOVE the person that I've become and the life that I've created as a result of what I learned during my time there. NOT being the same turned out to be a very good thing for me! And I LOVE how people have responded, connecting with my story and using it to empower their own.

Because the truths I learned there? Life-changing.

I still have the journal—green scrapbook paper sprinkled with white daisies hodge-podged to the cover—where Cornelia, my hospital social worker, challenged me to capture and dissect the rules of my childhood. Rules that, if left unchecked, would continue to impact me as a grown adult. (It's the same for all of us.)

The exercise was simple: Write down each of the main rules I followed, identify its purpose, and capture my emotional reaction.

So a few pages in, somewhere past "100 Faces +1" and "Wellness Recovery Action Plan" but before "How to become your own therapist" is a page titled, "What are the rules I had to follow as a child?" trailed by group after group of:

Rule:

Purpose:

Reaction:

It was there beneath reaction—between anger, grief, and sadness—that my greatest insights and discoveries were made.

"I had the right to know why," I wrote. "You drilled into my head that my voice didn't matter. No one wants to hear me. Your stupid rule had me suffocating. Now I carry heavy guilt when I don't just follow blindly. Why are their needs more important than mine? Doesn't God love me too?"

It was the first time I realized that *I* wasn't broken. The system was.

It was like inhaling for the first time after being too long under the water—both painful and exhilarating.

Then Cornelia had me turn to a new page.

"What do I write here?" I asked.

"The rules you want to live by now," she replied.

I stared dumbly. "You mean *I* get to pick?"

She nodded.

With a trembling hand I wrote, "#1 Live by your own set of rules."

That was the moment. The moment my life

changed. The moment I took control. The moment I chose ME and my life and my dreams.

And I never looked back.

Through the healing process I learned to define myself, set my own rules, claim what I wanted, and pursue my passions. I learned when to fight, when to nurture, and when to ask for help. I learned to trust my own voice and intuition. I learned to make my dreams non-negotiable and gave myself permission to make them happen *today* rather than waiting for someday.

And I learned that in being 100% authentic to myself and my dreams (along with pouring love and forgiveness into the world around me), that I empowered others to do the same.

Before the robbery, I'd resigned myself to a life that only partially filled me. I let "okay" be good enough and I told myself I was happy.

Today though—WOW!!! Because of that choice to invest in myself and my dreams, I am now living a Happily EPIC After where every day surpasses my wildest hopes and expectations!

You Deserve a Life that Fills You

After all that, how could I keep this Soul Song to myself? How could I NOT reach out and help others see that what they do, the gift they have, is needed in our world? How could I stay silent while fear and doubt continued to drown the other Soul Songs begging to be freed?

I couldn't. Even in the darkness of my post-hospital suicidality, my soul *knew* I needed to speak.

December 24, 2012:

"Death is the escape," I wrote. "But I don't really want death. I want more life. I want to travel. I want to see the world. I want to soak in experiences and places and words and life. I want to push that into my novels. I want my novels to sell and for more than just me to believe in the power of my words and characters. I want to speak with people who have faith transitions and to people who hate life and to victims of abuse and to people changed by trauma and I want to shout, 'YOU ARE GOOD ENOUGH! Keep going, give yourself what others refuse to or can't give you. Give yourself a chance. Pick a dream and then make it happen. It's going to be hard and you're going to want to give up, maybe every day, but you *can* make it happen. You can overcome. And when you do, the earth will not be able to contain your shine.' I want to change lives. I want to help others to find the awesome within. I want my life to mean something. I want to mean something."

I know that's what you want . . . to mean something. To create something that is bigger than you. To have your creation move across the Earth, impacting lives until the world cannot contain your shine!!!!!

But how do you do that . . . how do you run toward your greatness, follow your Soul Song and live your Happily EPIC After when you have fear, past failures, and current mental-gremlin obstacles standing in your way?

I'm here to show you.

Let's go!

BEHIND THE GLITTER:

Deb on the Comfort Zone

Q: How do I tell the difference between Fear and a HELL NO?

A: Ask yourself, "Why am I afraid?" Fear will answer with rationalizations (or irrationalizations if you're me). But HELL NO? It will give you a raised eyebrow and ask you why you're even questioning it. And it usually doesn't come with an excuse or explanation (until we give it one).

Which brings me to comfort zones. Let's chat that for a sec, shall we? Because you're about to not only step outside your comfort zone but *live* outside it. It's a side effect of choosing growth.

The cliff notes version . . . our brain treats the edge of our comfort zone as death. Try to step beyond the edge and all the alarm bells go off.

ARROOGAH ARROOGAH!!! Danger Will Robinson! It causes those rocks in our stomach, the sweaty palms, the increased heart rate, and more. You know what I'm talking about, right?

Put me in a group of people and ask me to engage in small talk and you might as well have dumped me in a cage surrounded by great white sharks! My brain reads this situation as death and gives me all sorts of ideas about running away and hiding. (My chest is getting tight just thinking about it!)

(This is awesome if I'm actually in the ocean and trying to avoid getting eaten. Not so great if I'm trying to meet new people, make new friends, or network for business.)

It will continue to feel like death until it doesn't anymore . . . a.k.a. until we've successfully established a *new* normal for our brain and system. (Which, for most people, would be the end.) For you and me? It starts all over again as we take *the next step* and the next and the next, each outside the comfort zone.

Bottom line? Fear will always be right there with us, riding in the back seat (as Elizabeth Gilbert likes to say). Which means we've gotta get comfortable living with it, and *really* good at distinguishing between it and that HELL NO.

So, keep paying attention to the intuitive hits you're getting and take action on them. Study what happens next. Know that you're going to make a mistake at some point and you will get the two confused. Learn from it and let it go.

And remember, HELL NOs don't need to be explained or excused.

You got this!

Have a question? Send me your insights and comments. I want to know what you think!
https://www.debbieburns.me/contact

CHAPTER TWO:

Ready or Not

LET'S GET INTO WHAT you came for. (Though I'm pretty sure you've already picked up some of the major diamonds I've dropped so far!)

We all have a true north sitting inside of us—our very own north star guiding our way. You can call her (or him!) your Inner Writer, Inner Artist, Inner Badass, Inner CEO, Inner God, Inner Goddess, Inner Creator . . . whatever you desire. It's this Higher Self that *knows* us intimately. Knows who we are, the gifts we have, and the power we hold. And she *knows* who we were designed to become before people and life experiences dimmed our light and silenced our Soul Songs.

We are drawn to her and she speaks to us, trying to amplify that purpose calling from our sacred place of creation. And yet, we tend to kind of push her down, silence her, put her at the back of the pack because we're afraid of what might happen if we truly lean into claiming our Big Dream.

What if we fail? What if we get rejected? What if, after all that work, nothing changes? And worse, what if we become wildly successful and get overwhelmed with the people, requests, and income?! How will we handle it? *Who* will we become? And what if we don't like Future Me?!!

AAAHHHHHH!!!!!!

Right? Tell me I'm not alone.

After teaching thousands of people and personally mentoring over a hundred, I see these same fears every time. Fears based in worn out truths (that are more like curses) handed down from well-meaning family, friends, teachers, leaders, and even strangers as we grow and interact with the world. Then something happens—we fail, fall down, get hurt, are rejected, feel shame—and our brain says, "See! I *knew* this was going to happen. Why didn't you just say no. I'm only trying to keep you safe."

And we learn to retreat rather than press forward. We learn to listen to the talking heads, constantly seeking belonging that is really just thinly veiled "fitting in." (And no, they are not the same.)

Then add to that the obstacles of growth, leadership, income, expenses, messaging, branding, marketing, and tribe-building as well as political, familial, and religious culture and you have a big old pot of Don't-take-another-step-forward Stew.

It tastes gross, but we eat it anyway and we tell ourselves we're happy.

Until now.

Because I'm about to blow your world open with *The Path to Courage*. And it starts with seven simple steps:

1. See through the fear
2. Separate who you are from what you do
3. Love who you are
4. Own your story
5. Choose your tribe over your fear
6. Follow the fireflies
7. Wash. Rinse. Repeat.

Go ahead and take a swig of water (you're going to need it), grab your Indian Jones whip, and let's get exploring!

BEHIND THE GLITTER:

Deb on Doubt

Q: What if I don't have what it takes to accomplish my Big Dream?

A: If you are *willing* to lean into your Soul Song, then you have what it takes to accomplish your Big Dream, EVEN IF you don't feel ready.

Let me put your heart at ease. You don't have to feel ready, okay? "Ready" is just a disguise for "I'm not perfect." Guess what? Nobody is! And the people you want to help? They don't want you to be perfect either. They want you to be real, faults and all, because they want to know that whatever your mission, message, product, call to arms . . . whatever it is you're bringing to the world . . . that it's all possible for them too!

If we keep waiting until we're ready, we'll never take the step. Because "ready" is a lie (just like perfection.) Good news/bad news . . . we are human!

The truth is we won't *ever* feel ready.

BUUUT!!!!—and that's a BIG BUT—we can feel *willing*.

Are you willing to serve? Willing to grow? Willing to try new things even if they scare you? Are you willing to give yourself permission to make mistakes, shake yourself off, and get back up again to make some more? And are you willing to give yourself grace through the process?

That willingness is enough to take those initial steps and develop the courage necessary to stand up, to shake things up, and to be seen.

And YOU, my friend, deserve to be seen!

So, if you are a sacred rebel *willing* to go deeper and be bolder and dream bigger—believing who you are inside here (*points to your heart*) has something greater to contribute out there (*points to the world*)—then we need to chat.

Have a question? Send me your insights and comments. I want to know what you think!
https://www.debbieburns.me/contact

CHAPTER THREE:

See through the Fear

I WAS A CHILD, maybe eight or nine, when I watched *IT* for the first (and only!) time. I'd finally been able to vanquish Mr. Boogedy (thanks for that one, Disney) and Freddy Krueger (hats off to you, Wes Craven) from my nightmares, but that damn clown? He hung on for *decades*, scaring me well into adulthood. (Tim Curry, I both admire and despise you for your role in this.)

I remember one nightmare vividly. Walking down a museum-like hall with glass enclosures on either side. Inside each display case was a different scene with Pennywise as its center piece. Pennywise as a grandma rocking in her chair. Pennywise as a farmer tending his pigs. Pennywise as a school teacher teaching her class, and so on. As I passed each case I saw his eyes follow me, his wicked grin showing razor-sharp teeth, and with my mind I remember setting the contents of each display on fire.

At the end of the hallway was the enclosure with Pennywise as himself. Terrifying and bigger than life.

And no glass.

With fires burning behind me, I looked up at him and screamed, "You're not real! And you can't hurt me!!!"

He leaned down, teeth glinting in the low light. "I am very real. And I can hurt you."

I woke, fear pounding in my chest.

There are a LOT of things we could take from that dream, but we'll save therapy time for another day. Instead, I share this dream because I believe this is how Fear (with a capital F) often shows up in our life. We *see* it. We *know* it's there! But regardless of how much we tell ourselves it isn't real, it still seems more powerful than the logic of our brain or the faith of our soul. It seems to say, "I am very real. And I *can* hurt you."

That is why we stop, give up, don't try, run away, and even hide.

Are we really going to die if we get on stage and mess up? Nope! But we still avoid it. Are we really going to die if we do a livestream and tumble over our words? Not a chance. But we still put if off (and off and off and off). Are we really going to die if we tell people our truth and live by our own set of rules? It may feel like it at the time! But I'm here as proof that no, we don't have to die in order to truly live.

You might be wondering, then, how do we stop the fear?

The answer is, we don't.

We see *through* it.

This is step number one on our path to courage. But *how* do we do that, right? Here's what I want you to do:

On a piece of paper (one that you are willing to throw away) I want you to answer the question, "What is holding me back? What is getting in the way of what I want to accomplish?"

Don't over think this. Just write. I'll wait.

plays Jeopardy music

Got it? Cool!

Whatever you wrote on your paper, I want you to know you are not alone. How can I say that? Because I've been watching the people in my tribe, I've been keeping track of the fears and obstacles standing in their way, and I see the same core issues show up every time:

- I'm afraid of failing.
- I'm afraid of succeeding.
- I'm afraid I am not enough.
- I'm afraid my story isn't enough.
- I don't have enough time.
- My family expects me to do something else.
- My Soul Song doesn't make money or feed my family.
- I lack the focus.
- I have low self-esteem, confidence, or don't believe in myself.
- Competing priorities.
- Money money money money money.
- Perfection.
- I need to do or get XYZ first.
- And more.

There is no right or wrong here. It's solely about identifying what's getting in *your* way, so whatever you wrote down is great! It's your starting point.

Once you have that on your piece of paper, I want you to dive deeper. To look *through* the initial answer to the underlying cause. Ask yourself, "Why is this in my way? What's beneath that excuse?

What is the underlying fear? What is really holding me back?"

Let me give you a real-life example from one of my clients, Andrea. We'd discussed fear in our first in-depth appointment and this same process for overcoming. (And let me tell you, she is AMAZING in her willingness to shine a light in the dark places! Love her insights!) Weeks later, I received this message from her:

> *I was thinking about the Wrap & Reset post this morning and acknowledged that I haven't set specific goals for myself. When I asked myself why, I got the answer that I'm afraid/worried/concerned that I won't hit my goal(s).*
>
> *So I asked myself why again. I'm afraid of the things I can't see coming. Like snow days (which means my kids are home and it makes it more difficult to get things done), for example.*
>
> *So then I asked myself, "so what?" What would happen if I didn't hit my goals? They're something to strive for, not a standard by which to measure my worth.*

And there it was! The *real* fear buried beneath all the excuses. Andrea was afraid that if she didn't reach her goals, somehow that would mean she didn't have worth. She continued:

If I'm not hitting my goals, maybe I'm not setting realistic ones and my goals need to be evaluated and adjusted. That doesn't diminish my worth. If anything, this awareness reinforces my self-worth.

My goal for this coming week is to do at least two 20-minute sprints per day, at least five days this week.

I love how seeing through her fear empowered Andrea to take steps forward toward her Soul Song. When we strip away the excuse, what we really find is a deeper fear preventing us from taking action.

My excuse comes back again and again to time management. When I start hearing myself say, "I don't have enough time," I know that what I'm really saying is, "I don't believe I'm worth it." That's the deeper fear *behind* time issues . . . that I am not worth the time investment required to sing my Soul Song.

For many, it comes down to love and belonging—the fear of showing your true self and having that truth, that inner core, rejected. For others it's about worthiness, security, or avoiding shame. For you, maybe it is a fear that you're not good enough or that, after all is said and done, you won't be successful anyway.

Keep asking yourself, "Why is this blocking me? What am I REALLY afraid of?" until you find the core. Because here's the deal . . . we can't deal with the fear unless we are willing to shine a light on it.

Once upon a time, my husband and I were startled awake in the middle of the night by a loud clang. We thought someone had broken into our house. It was the most terrifying thing ever (up to that point in our lives, anyway). We had no weapons, so I grabbed a curtain rod that we hadn't hung up yet—you know, one of those flimsy, easily breakable kinds—and we stalked from room to room clearing the house (honestly, we didn't know what we were doing).

Finally, we got to the garage and I won't ever forget opening the door. I was terrified, heart pounding in my chest, throat tight with an unspoken scream. *Anything* could be behind that door and I imagined the worst as I reached for the handle. I yanked it open as my husband jumped inside (still in his underwear!), the curtain rod lifted high above his head and ready to strike!!! (In hindsight, it was hysterical!)

With the light on, what we discovered was that the spring on the big garage door had broken and popped off, causing the crashing noise that had woken us up. Nothing even remotely close to the worst-case scenarios I had conjured in my head! But I'll remember that feeling of fear forever and ever.

I think the same thing happens with our growth. We feel afraid of something and we don't want to turn on the light, because what if we *do* turn it on and the scary clown with the chainsaw is actually there?!

So we ignore it. We look a different way. Or we keep trying to solve for a time management problem when what we really have is a worthiness problem.

My friend, unless we turn on the light, unless we're willing to step into that garage, we won't know the truth of what we're dealing with.

Only when we truly look can we start targeting the *real* problem and actually see lasting progress. In my case, I solved my Pennywise nightmares when I found the deeper issue hiding beneath and healed that. And I continue to solve each layer of the time management problem as I solve the deeper and deeper layers of my Inner Goddess / Artist / Writer / Badass / CEO one.

Whatever your fear is, be willing to at least turn the light on so you can not only see it, you can see through it.

Let's pause for just a sec, okay? If you are feeling overwhelmed right now, take a deep breath. You don't have to go insanely deep at this point in time if it is too much to do on your own. One of my gifts is being able to feel the deeper truth—in both Soul Songs and fears—so I tend to dive deep very quickly. If this is too deep too fast, don't worry, pull back and just look for that first thing underneath your block, okay?

So, on your piece of paper you should have whatever is getting in your way *plus* the fear hiding underneath (as deep as you want to go).

Got it? Sweet! Now set that aside. (I promise, we'll circle back to it later, so don't lose it!) For now, we need to keep moving on our path to courage.

Step one, we identify *why* we're running away—which you've just done . . .

And step two, we separate who we are from what we do.

Are you in?

BEHIND THE GLITTER:

Deb on Rejection

Q: What if I embrace my truest self and people don't like me?

A: When you live as your truest self, you *draw* your truest people. And, I promise, they will love you!

One of the things that I realized while I was in the hospital was that I was *terrified* of people seeing the true me. What if I pulled away all of the masks I was wearing and my one, truest face was too ugly for others?

I think this is a huge fear for many of us who are awakening to our Soul Song, especially if we've spent most of our lives trying to be what others want us to be. I can't sugar coat this. *Some* people will pull away. They won't like the changes you're making. They'll disagree with your choice into growth. And things will feel wonky for a period of time.

BUT, I also know that the closer you live to *your* true north, the more powerful your relationships will become. Because they choose you *for you*. They love you *for you*. They admire you *for you*. And they follow you *because of you*. That, my friend, is powerful.

Have a question? Send me your insights and comments. I want to know what you think!
https://www.debbieburns.me/contact

CHAPTER FOUR:

Separate Who You Are from What You Do

TRAVERSING PTSD HAS BEEN a difficult, yet fascinating experience. I'm not gonna be the girl who tells you everything happens for a reason. Nope. I didn't ask this guy to rob me, break my brain, and send me spiraling into the abyss. *However*, I do believe we can learn something from every experience. There is a takeaway in every moment if we're willing to look for it.

While in the hospital, I was not willing. I wanted to blame and hate and be angry, which was totally cool. We need time to actually feel our emotions, to explore them and just *be* with them. I took that time. And a year or so later, I found myself looking back on that experience in surprise. (Truth be told, I'm *still* learning from the fallout of that trauma.)

Because in a moment of pure clarity I realized an insane, amazing, heart-pounding

**truth: I didn't end up suicidal because some-
one else had threatened to take my life. I ended
up suicidal because, *after* he had threatened to
take my life, I couldn't be the person others ex-
pected me to be.**

BOOM!

mind explodes

Before the robberies (I probably forgot to
mention, but yes it happened twice about seven
weeks apart), I was *the* girl that everyone went to
for everything. Projects, opinions, last minute requests, service opportunities, mediation help and
more—you name it, I probably had someone asking me to help them with it. I could balance twenty-
plus things at the same time, was super articulate,
and well respected by family, friends, and col-
leagues. Sure, I was unhappy and stressed, but hey!
Look at all the stuff I could do! I had SO MUCH
WORTH!!!!

And then, suddenly, I couldn't do *any* of those
things anymore. I lost vocabulary words (even having to pantomime the word "iron" on several oc-
casions because I simply could not remember the
word)! I lost my ability to hold one project at a
time, let alone a ton of them. I tried to keep working, traumatizing myself over and over again while

my production levels went down. I pulled away from all external events and hid from the world. People didn't even get a "no" from me, they just got silence. And I started wondering, "What's the point of me? I can't do this or that. I can't complete the checklist. I can't even remember the word 'iron' for crying out loud!!!"

I fell behind in work first, then church, then life responsibilities until one day that beautifully shiny, black Glock was so enticing I couldn't resist anymore. That knife in the kitchen. That rope in the laundry bags. Joe's tie hanging in the closet . . .

If I couldn't keep up, if I couldn't check all the boxes on all the lists that had been piled up in front of me over the years, then maybe it would be better to relieve this planet of such a waste of space.

(I type that now and I want to cry out to my old self, "Of course you matter!" I'm just glad I know she knows that now.)

It was a hard climb out of the abyss, but one of the most important things I learned through that process was to separate WHO I was from WHAT I could do. And I want to show you how to do the same for yourself.

Pull out a new piece of paper because, right now in this moment, you're gonna start claiming who you are. (Make sure it's separate from the "fears" paper you just wrote on.)

Your "who" is made up of qualities and characteristics, not actions and roles. And I want your brain to see this in action. While we could go several different directions with this, for this specific exercise, I just want you to focus on the *positive* qualities and characteristics that make up who you are. Number your paper from 1 to 100 (nope, that's not a typo . . . I really mean 1-0-0) and write down every word that pops in your head. If you think it, write. (If it's negative word, write it on the back of your "fears" paper.)

Want a one-page worksheet that already has the numbers laid out for you? I got you, boo! Go to www.sacredrebels.me/100words for your free PDF download. Glitter Tip: I do this exercise at least twice a year as a check-up for my headspace.

Now, roles will come up for you, and if a role comes up for you, you're okay to add it to your list, but then I want you to take the time to break that role down. If "mom" comes up for you first, you would write:

1.   Mom

(Then you would break that apart into the positive qualities and characteristics that define "mom" *for you*. That might look like . . .)

2. Creative
3. Big heart
4. Nurturing
5. Dedicated

And so on. Same goes if you write down anything like, "sister, friend, auntie, daughter, teacher, leader" etc.

Just to clarify . . . being any and all of those things is really, really great! This isn't about discounting the things that we do in our life. It's about seeing them as separate.

Roles are *what we do*. The qualities that make up that role? That is *who we are*.

If we entrench our identity in the doing, then when that thing is taken away from us, we enter crisis—like the mom who becomes an empty nester, the CEO badass who loses her job, the artist who is struggling to "catch her break," and more.

I want to show you that as a writer, when I put down my pen and I step out of this room (or if, heaven forbid, there comes a point where writing isn't a part of my life anymore), I still get to take all the qualities of "writer" with me—creative, intelligent, imaginative, fun, provocative, etc.—into the role of being wife, friend, sibling, daughter, teacher, leader, and so on. I get to be creative in whatever I'm doing! I get to be intelligent in whatever hat I wear! I get to be fun in whatever thing I'm teaching!

Now I get to be all of those amazing things in *all* the roles, not just one.

So do you!

Okay, back to your list. I want to make sure you are numbering each positive quality, characteristic, and role. Why? Because the analytical side of your brain requires data for "proof" that something is true. Numbers (especially in this list format) resonate as data to the analytical side, which then sends a signal to the creative side telling it, "This is true! We're amazing! Keep creating!" It is imperative to have those numbers next to every positive trait.

Again, if negative words come up, just write them on the back of your "fears" paper.

This will be work, especially as you pass 20, 50, and 75. There is a reason I push you to go to 100! Because we want to get to the really delicious words. The ones buried beneath some of our more flippant, "Yeah. I'm smart. So what?" responses.

Keep going, even when it gets hard. Ask valued friends and family if you need more words. One epic resource is to take all those negative words (a.k.a. words that no longer serve you) and write their opposite on your paper. Meaning, if you wrote, "too much" on the other paper, you could write "just right" or "super fun" or "entertaining" on the 100-word list I've asked you to create. This helps you tap into what your Higher Self knows to be true, even if your conscious mind is rejecting it right now. And if you see a trait you admire in someone else, it means that you have it inside you, so grab those words too!

At the end of the day it comes down to this: The things that we do are the hats that we put on our head, but the qualities and characteristics we claim are part of *who we are*. Truths that we can carry with us through any identity, through any role, through anything that we do on this planet— we can be those things!

When I was lost and alone and ready to take my life, I was still loving. I was still empathetic. I was still compassionate and caring. I was still creative. I was still all of those things.

All of these positive traits that you've written down? These are all of *your* things.

This is just the start. Let me say that again . . . *This is just the start.* I'm actually going to challenge you to keep adding to this list. Keep adding and don't stop. Every time you see a trait that resonates with you or that you want, write it down. Claim it. Your fun may look different than my fun, but it's inside of you.

One last piece to be aware of . . . pay attention to how you define a word. As long as it means something positive to you, keep it. Stubborn can make some people feel awful while others love it! If a word makes you feel shame (or it's an excuse for non-aligned behavior), it's not serving you. Get rid of it. If you're not sure, double check your definition. To me, "stubborn" is awesome! It means I'm stubborn in following my dream, stubborn in the defense of my family, stubborn in helping my clients see their truest self, etc.

If there's a word that comes up and you need more clarity, write out the definition (perhaps on the back or your list). Then *your* brain knows, "Oh, this is what we mean when we say the word stubborn, or when we say the word fun or high-energy." Then it doesn't matter how anyone else defines that word. *You* know. And you know that your definition serves you.

My friend, treasure these words. They are a gift of truth! Keep the ones that are serving you and release the ones that aren't. You are worth it.

You. Are. Worth it.

I love this exercise so much. It's foundational in the work I do and powerful as we walk the path to courage. Because this is what helps us to take the next step.

Now that we've seen through our fear and separated who we are from what we do, we can move forward into loving who we are.

Need some words? Dedicated, smart, loving, compassionate, kind, brilliant, empathetic, saucy, adventurous, passionate, vivacious, loyal, outgoing, enduring, creative, insightful, forgiving, uplifting, determined, focused, talented, wise, calm, pleasant, sweet, worthy, whole, complete, friendly, innovative, fun, courageous, light, sunshine, fire-forged.

BEHIND THE GLITTER:

Deb on Mistakes

Q: Why should I let go of the negative stuff? Aren't my mistakes a part of me?

A: They are as much a part of you as the poop you push out on the daily. So, if you're keeping that, then by all means, keep the negative mental chatter too.

Our bodies are naturally designed to release the stuff that it no longer needs. Hence the pooping. The same goes for our mental space—only we have to *manually* take out the waste. Negative self-talk, whether introduced to us via others' words or via our own thoughts and actions, only makes the system sick if we hold onto it.

Our job is to learn from whatever we experience (things that happen to us, things that are said to us, or choices we've made ourselves, both helpful and not helpful), and let the rest go. Think of it like the healthy digestion of food where we keep the "nutrients" and release the "waste." Our mistakes, failures and past stories are just food. Receive the nutrient (a.k.a. the takeaway of whatever experience) and let the rest go.

The problem comes when we start seeing ourselves as the food—a.k.a. *I am* the failure, *I am* the mistake, *I am* the bad thing that happened to me, or *I am* the bad thing I chose to do . . .

. . . Rather than the system *digesting* the food—a.k.a. I am a great person who *had* a failure, I am a kind person who *made* a mistake, I am a loving human and something bad *happened to me*, or I am an intelligent person who *made* a bad choice.

When we aren't careful about taking the mental garbage out, we run the risk of believing the lie that we are what we do.

So! The old traits that aren't helping you get where you want to go? Release them.

Former actions that turned into mistakes and failures? Learn from them.

Harmful words or actions used against you? Forgive them.

Whatever you do, please don't let those "things that no longer serve you" continue to influence who you think you can be and what you can accomplish going forward.

It *is* possible to be more powerful than the negative self-talk and mental gremlins, even if you can only see your failures and mistakes right now.

Want to feel empowered to follow your Soul Song without worrying about being rejected because of your past failures and mistakes? Let the Sacred Rebels tribe help you. Become a member: www.sacredrebels.me.

Have a question? Send me your insights and comments. I want to know what you think!
https://www.debbieburns.me/contact

CHAPTER FIVE:

Love Who You Are

OKAY, THE SUSPENSE is killing me!!! I've got to know what you put on your 100-word list!!!

Take a sec and pop on over to my Facebook biz page and, using hashtag #pathtocourage, share some of your words with me. Not only does that give me a chance to love on you, it allows your words to help another sacred rebel who is looking to empower her list. Woot!!!! I love how we can all lift each other! https://www.facebook.com /debbersxoxo

Cool! Let's keep going!

Now that you've captured all those beautiful words, we want to strengthen the connection between you and the building blocks of who you are. (Let's be honest. It's one thing to write them, it's a different thing entirely to *believe* them.)

And we're going to do that with a little thing called repetition and intensity.

Loving who you are is a daily practice. It's not a light switch and it definitely doesn't happen overnight. It's not a destination either. You're not going to arrive at self-love and—Poof!—magically never doubt yourself again. It doesn't work that way.

It goes back to growth and the comfort zone. Just as you'll always be expanding into new fears, you'll also be expanding into new levels of self-love.

For now, though, I want you to get comfortable with the list you just created. This means making a few copies and posting them where you're going to see them—*often.* I recommend putting a copy:

- Right by your bed so you can read through it before you go to sleep at night and when you wake up in the morning. It's a great exercise to fill your mind with your awesomeness before dreaming! Let your mind percolate on that all night (instead of all the things you have to do the next day.)

- In your purse so when mental gremlins strike on the commuter train or in the grocery store, you can read through your list and remind yourself that you have 100+ data points that prove those gremlins are liars.

- On your bathroom mirror so you can remind yourself how worthy you are as you brush your teeth or handle that hair.

- By your computer at work so you can remember that your amazing qualities are useful at work, at home, and as a part of any role you play.

Where else could you post this where you'll see it all the time? (I do *not* recommend taping them to the inside of your car windshield. Safety first!)

You could also snap a picture to keep them on your phone or make something creative (like a screen saver!) to remind you of your greatness.

The point is to refer back to this list often, multiple times a day, so that you can fall in love with your amazingness again and again and again. And before you get all twisted up about claiming your greatness, let me set the record straight: *It's okay to toot your own horn!* It's okay to own your greatness. This isn't about being better than other people. It's about loving yourself *as much* as you love them.

When we truly love ourselves, we have the capacity to truly love other people without

comparison and hierarchy. We can accept at our core that being fire-forged isn't any better or worse than being compassionate, which isn't any better or worse than being powerful, eloquent, motivational, extrovert, introvert, or calm. Okay?

Now that we've covered repetition (a.k.a. reading your list daily), let's talk intensity!

To really kick this transformation up a notch, I want you to say your words out loud with "I love that I am . . ." in front of each one. So, a list of "kind, adorable, fun, creative, whole," would turn into: "I love that I am kind. I love that I am adorable. I love that I am fun. I love that I am creative. I love that I am whole."

You can also group a few together. Do what feels good to you. For example: "I love that I am dedicated and empathetic and loyal. I love that I am intelligent and giving and whole."

When you wake up in the morning, you do the same thing. You tell yourself how much you love these qualities and characteristics about you, because they are beautiful and they are wonderful and they are the things that are going to keep you going when mental gremlins, family members, well-meaning friends, and horrible trolls try to step up and stomp you out.

It's a daily practice of showing up for yourself, claiming your truths and expressing love for who you are.

I know this work is powerful and it is deep! If you are having any insights, breakthroughs, or light bulbs going on, I would love to know! Share them with me via email: hello@debbieburns.me

---

Okay, so that was step three, love who you are. Now we'll get into the deliciousness that is owning your story!

BEHIND THE GLITTER:

Deb on the Art of Selfing

Q: I keep falling back into the same patterns. Why isn't this working?

A: Remember—whether we're talking transformation, courage, living your Soul Song, or being true to you—change happens as we *keep* taking steps. You only truly fail when you stop trying (and that's only if you still want whatever it was you were trying to achieve).

I call it the art of selfing. Just like how we learn to swim by swimming and run by running, we learn to become our best self by selfing! It's a process of *practice*, not instantaneous and miraculous change. Which means we are gonna try and try and try to hold the pattern of this higher way of being and, eventually, we are gonna "fall" or "fail."

When that happens, instead of hating on or beating ourselves up, we simply use it as an opportunity to realign (a.k.a. line back up) with the true self we want to become. So we go, "Oh, oh, oh, oh, I'm pointing at *someone else's* north star. That's not where I want to be," or "Ooops! I acted out of alignment by being unkind. I'm just going to step back to *my* true north." Boom, done! Realigned.

It's all about choosing to realign with the Higher Self that you want to be *as often as it takes*. Any time you get off track, you just have to step back on the path.

You take radical responsibility for you. Allow others to take radical responsibility for them. Apologize when necessary. And keep trying to be the best version of you on the daily. Alignment is actually quite simple, though not always easy.

So your mistakes and failures? They mean you are trying. They are an indicator that you are on the path and that you can do even better! And as you keep practicing . . . as you keep selfing . . . you'll be able to see the progress (regardless of how big or small.)

Struggling to reveal the true you? Not sure what "authentic" looks like? I'm here to help. We explore your Soul Song and the deeper doubts and fears getting in your way in the Sacred Rebels membership. Go to: www.sacredrebels.me.

Have a question? Send me your insights and comments. I want to know what you think!

https://www.debbieburns.me/contact

CHAPTER SIX:

Own Your Story

WHEREVER YOU'VE COME FROM, however you got here, whatever drew you to follow your Soul Song and choose your Big Dream, I encourage you to own that story.

Way too often I see visionary people (myself included) get in this trap of comparison:

- "She has been doing XYZ since the beginning."
- "She is already talking about what makes my heart sing! There's no room for me."
- "She is such a better speaker."
- "She has already been on BIG NAME media outlet. How can I compete?"

Which leads to . . .

- "What about me?"
- "Where do I fit?"

- "I'm not X enough or Y enough or Z enough. There is no place for me."

And before we've even begun the journey, we've given up.

Maybe you've been there? Maybe you find yourself there now? Whatever the case, I want you to own your story starting right now. Make it a part of your brand, a part of your journey! Embrace where you've come from, focusing on the strengths to build credibility and on the heartaches to create connection.

We all start somewhere. Many of us begin in the mess, that we turn into learning, that transforms into healing, that becomes the message, business or product that we want to share with the world.

I have a client, Cindy, a fabulous, heart-centered creator and yarn dyer from Europe. I've worked with her business for over a year now, helping her strategically with product launches, client concerns, and achieving set goals. As we entered into this new year, Cindy asked me if we could focus on what makes her unique, what sets her apart from others in her industry. When she looked at this designer or that dyer, she could tell, immediately, what made them different. And she wanted to have that for herself.

Of course, I said yes. I already *knew* what made her shine!

As we talked through our first quarterly planning meeting of the year it became even more apparent. It was there, in her story.

She loved to create colors for her yarn based on memories and feelings. Every color has a story—either hers or her clients—that becomes visual art that others can then knit into their own creation. This color was Christmas last year. That one was spring peeking through winter. And that other one . . . in the purple hues . . . based on Amethyst to elevate the soul and assist with transformation. Incredible, right? (She even created a color just for me!!! Glitter cannon—a stripped yarn in pink and purple hues and splashed with glitter! I love it!)

But it doesn't stop there. She also desires to create a tighter connection between fiber artists in her area. She wants collaboration and community, which goes against the norms of her culture. If you look at her story, not only in business but in her personal life as well, you see the craving for connection, the big heart that desires to help, the love that shines through everything she does, the tenderness with which she approaches the world, and a desire to lead by example.

It's all there, inside her story.

So how does she own this? She works it into her business conversations and social media posts. She adds it to her website. She highlights her *why* (capturing memories and creating community) as she talks to people about her *what* (yarn dying). And she uses her stories behind each color to inspire the fiber artists looking for yarn as she uses her desire for collaboration (and the ups and downs of working against cultural norms) to create more connection in her on- and offline communities.

My friend, there is *power* in being able to claim our story and say:

- "Hey, I didn't start doing XYZ until my 30's. I can kick ass at this and do some amazing things."
- "I conquered XYZ in my 20's. I can kick ass at this and do amazing things."
- "I didn't start anything until my 50's, 60's, 70's. I can still kick ass and do amazing things."

Because once we claim our story, no one can use it against us. It becomes a mountain that we can stand on, rather than a tar pit we get stuck in.

My story is mine and it is what I will use to write my journey. Your story is yours and it is beautiful and fabulous and what you will use to create your journey. Just don't let the past dictate who you can become in the future, okay?

One of my favorite coaches, Jennifer Kem, (inspired by Lisa Nichols) says it this way, "Don't sit in your story, stand on your story." Claim it, but don't get stuck, don't get buried up to your neck in your story, okay?

We've seen through our fear, separated who we are from what we do, we've talked about loving who we are via our 100-word lists, and we've explored owning our stories. Now we're really getting to the good stuff!!! (What am I saying?! It's ALL good stuff!!!!) The next step on the path to courage is to choose your tribe over your fear.

BEHIND THE GLITTER:

Deb on Feeling like a Fraud

Q: I don't feel like I fit into my industry. Am I a fraud?

A: I'll give you the same advice my mentor and coach, Jennifer Kem, gave to me, "Every industry needs a sacred rebel."

We sat around the table, seven women from various business and life backgrounds, sharing what struggles we were having in our business.

"My industry doesn't want me," I shared. "I don't look like the main players. I don't speak like them. And I'm definitely saying things that aren't playing by the rules."

That's when Jen held up an oracle card and said, "Every industry needs a sacred rebel." (Doesn't that just make you tingle?!) Her words resonated in me, straight down to my bones.

As I write this book, those words make me think of you.

Because you and I don't exist to make the mainstream feel more comfortable. We don't exist to regurgitate the same damn answers that have been tumbling around in our industries for years. We don't exist to prove the "gurus" right or to validate the talking heads.

We exist because our industries need a kick in the pants! (How hard I will leave up to you.) We exist because there are people out there asking the Universe for something more. We exist because a Higher Power, Higher Force, Higher Call planted within us a sacred purpose and it's asking us to step up, show up, be seen, be counted, and be *the change* that is needed in this part of the world.

We exist not to placate, but to challenge! Not to conform, but to explore!!!

Every industry needs someone who can wake up and shake up those who are already craving the insights, wisdom, and transformation you can provide.

You are that sacred rebel. *You* are that answered prayer. *You* are the one capable of creating *that thing* that will change hearts and minds.

You are not a fraud, but a revolutionary.

It's okay to stand up and stand out. It's okay to be different. It's okay to call out the dissonance and show people a different way. It's okay to define your new way of belonging and then call those people to you who want what you have to offer.

You won't convince everyone. You don't have to. You just have to stand up for those who are already waiting for the gift you have to share.

Have a question? Send me your insights and comments. I want to know what you think!
https://www.debbieburns.me/contact

CHAPTER SEVEN:

Choose Your Tribe over Your Fear

COURAGE IS AN ACTION. And I'm not talking about living without fear. It's not fearlessness. We wake up and we're afraid every single day. We're afraid of people, we're afraid of situations, we're afraid of things going wrong, and we're afraid of things going right. We're afraid of being too much, not enough, and everything in between all at the same time.

Courage isn't living without fear, it is the ability to take action *in spite* of fear. It's being willing to feel the fear, puke glitter, and do it anyway.

One "trick" to feeling emboldened is to remember the people you serve (a.k.a. your tribe) and to *choose them* over the fear of online (and even real-life) trolls speaking up, being unkind, or even hating what we've done. Mother Theresa had haters. Ellen DeGeneres, Oprah Winfrey, Michelle

Obama, Emma Watson, J.K. Rowling . . . all of them (and more!) have had their share of trolls spreading the hate.

Every visionary in the history of the world, whether religious or secular, has dealt with haters. We live on a planet of over 7 billion people, all with different opinions, backgrounds, beliefs, and more, so we can't expect to avoid the un-fans. It's just not possible. At some point or other you will have someone, perhaps several someones, try to call you out or put you down because they don't like how you show up in the world.

I love the way my friend and coach, Lynne Maureen Hurdle (the Conflict Closer), puts it. She said to me, "Deb, treat conflict like the zombie apocalypse. You prepare for it to happen, but you don't wait by the door, opening it every few seconds to see if a zombie is there." (Hehehe, she knows me so well!)

Trolls are not a matter of if, my friend, they are a matter of when and we've got to be prepared. When we put our Soul Song into the world, we are actually opening ourselves up to be vulnerable, and that can be a very, very scary process.

Here's the trick: focus on your people. Focus on the members of your tribe. Focus on the person that you showed up to do this big work for. Focus on them.

Anytime I find myself afraid to hit the publish button—like sending a newsletter that's a little edgy, publishing a post that doesn't follow with the mainstream, etc.—I have to sit there in that moment and ask myself, "Who am I writing this for?"

Because if I'm writing it just to be smart and witty, I haven't done my job. It's not our job to wow people with our intelligence. Our job as creators, leaders, Big Dreamers, is to be honest and real. To move something in someone else, to evoke emotion, an experience. To help them believe that something different, something better is possible than the reality they live right now.

When I write, share, speak, or do anything for my Debbie Burns brand, I'm thinking of you. Seriously. Even right now as I type these words, your face is in my mind. I'm thinking about you, about the struggles you have, about the desires that set your soul on fire, and I'm asking myself, "Will this help her? Will it answer something that's been plaguing her for a while? Will it support her, uplift her, strengthen her, remind her she is powerful and her work is needed in this world?"

If I can answer yes, I hit publish.

Because I am committed to choosing my tribe—YOU—over the trolls and over the fear that someone along the way is going to get offended by what I say. We cannot control someone else's offense. We can only speak our truth in a way that is in alignment with our highest self.

So, let your Soul Song come out of you and focus your energies and your efforts on the people, the movement, the message and let that matter *more* than the haters.

You matter. Your voice matters. Your tribe matters.

Trolls? Oh my great googley mooglies! They're going to be here and gone. Let's stop feeding the trolls and start choosing our tribe over the fear.

Here's what I want you to do. On your positive word list, I want you to write one thing that you haven't done because of fear. It can be anything. It can be, "wear my crazy socks outside," "share one of my truths on social media," "talk about my story," etc.

Pick just one thing that you have been hesitating to do because of fear. And you know what I'm going to ask you to do, right? (Because I already told you, this step is all about action.)

Do that thing. Do it now, today. Do it for the tribe you desire to serve. Be bold for them and it will help you be bold for you.

I'd love to know how it went! What action did you take and how did you feel afterward? Send me an email and let me know your story: hello@debbieburns.me.

Squeee!!!! My booty is shakin' right now in anticipation of what you're about to do! Taking a courageous action is SO energizing!!!

dances on the bed

You can do it! Remember, feel the fear, puke glitter, and do it anyway. Can't wait!!!

BEHIND THE GLITTER:

Deb on Belonging

Q: What should I be looking for in a powerful, healthy tribe?

A: You're looking to add three "categories" of people to your tribe, all built on a strong foundation of belonging—defined as "you invested in them and they invested in you."

First, you want **mentors and coaches**. These are the people who have been where you are and who are where you want to be. They've traveled the road, whether 10 or 100 steps in front of you, they understand your struggles and they know how to get you over, around, though, and under the myriad of booby traps along the way.

Best way to find these people is to understand your own gaps first. Where do you need help? What do you feel is missing? Who can help you solve that? Then listen to your intuition, understanding that just because a coach is AMAZING in *one* thing, it doesn't make them the expert in *all* things. Don't put them on that pedestal and be okay releasing them if and when the time comes.

Next, you want **peers**. These are the people around the same part of the journey as you, give or take a step. These are your fireflies who will encourage, love, support, cheer, and otherwise help you reach that finish line. Look for peers who have really great energy and a positive, can do, "we got this" outlook on life. And make sure you are that kind of peer and friend in return. These are the people you will learn from, grow with, celebrate, cry over, and help carry when they can't take one more step. These are the people who will do the same for you.

Finally, you'll gather your **audience**. These are the people who you've been called to serve via your Soul Song and Big Dream! You will be *their* light and the answer to *their* gap. (Glitter Tip: Don't get "serve" mixed up with "free." Give-receive is a necessary part of transformation. Don't rob your tribe of their power by devaluing yours.)

When you are willing to be the kind of leader, peer, and tribe member you desire to find, step up and be amazed by who the Universe sends your way.

Have a question? Send me your insights and comments. I want to know what you think!
https://www.debbieburns.me/contact

CHAPTER EIGHT:

Follow the Fireflies

STORY TIME! FOLLOW ME on this because I swear these are going somewhere. *wink wink*

Spider Crickets

Once upon a time, I was a leader at a girls' camp. Now, it's taken me a long time in my life to discover that I don't actually like the outdoors. Growing up, I was like, "Oh, I'm such a camper! I love camping! Trailers are for whimps, blah blah blah!" But the older I get, the more my idea of camping has become a beautiful cabin on the edge of the wilderness where I can enjoy nature (on a path or from my porch) and return home to a hot shower and a real toilet. That's important to me.

Yet there I was, trying to be strong, at this really great girls' camp up in the Pennsylvania mountains somewhere. Sure, they had flushing toilets and hot showers (or that would have been a straight up HELL NO!), but we slept in little cabins out and away from all the amenities of modern life.

One night, after snapping off the flashlights, we heard screaming from one of the most distant cabins. The whole situation was already a horror movie in the making, but when you're the adult, what do you do? So my co-leader and I jumped out of bed and raced toward the screams where we found some of the girls from said horror cabin already running toward us, yelling our names.

They were screaming, the remaining girls in the cabin were screaming, people from all over were waking up . . . it was a mess. And getting them to calm down once we finally arrived at the cabin was a bit of a joke.

Keeping my cool I said, "Okay, shh, what's going on? Somebody explain it to me, what's happening?"

Several girls at once, "There is a BUG! Ah!"

I replied, "Oh, okay, so everybody calm down, just be calm. It's fine." Even though it was definitely *not* fine. One of the girls was hyperventilating—she didn't do bugs—and I was wishing I *could* hyperventilate because I did not do bugs either. But, hey, I'm the adult so I tried to calm her down and keep everything chill. My co-leader took door duty, sending other campers back to their beds while I began pulling blankets apart, looking for the insect.

Friend, by this point I was terrified. Did I mention I don't like bugs? Yes? Well . . . let me say it again . . . I. Do NOT. Do. Bugs!

But I had to keep my cool, right? Because I'm the leader, I'm the adult here. So I was keeping my cool, moving blankets apart to try and find this bug as I kept telling the girls, "We're just going to grab it and we're going to put it outside."

And then I pushed these blankets apart . . .

And HOOOOLYYYY SHIIIIIIIZNIT!!!!

flails Kermit arms

There, between the folds, was this bug . . . the biggest, ugliest spider-looking bug I have ever seen on the planet!!!!

(I do not do bugs, but spiders are their own special brand of HELL NO!)

In that moment I made the mistake of moving. It jumped, I screamed, and the cabin went nuts.

And I didn't even care! That thing was terrifying. I swear it tried to kill me. It flew straight at my face!!!

A SPIDER. That FLEW! AT MY FACE!!!

No god ever should have made flying spiders;

they are bad enough without wings! But there it was . . . this *thing* . . . and it *flew*, and I started screaming, and the girls started screaming, "Mrs. Burns, you lied to us!!!" The cabin went nuts.

And all I could do was scream.

So anyway, poor girl, the one that hyperventilated, I am pretty sure she had a coronary. It was bad. But eventually we got the bug out. Well . . . someone else got the bug out, because I wasn't about to deal with no spider cricket.

You East Coasters, it is wrong. I don't know what's going on over there, but your bugs are bigger, they're scarier, and they're more colorful. I lived in Maryland for four years, and I don't plan on going back because of the bugs.

Someone eventually got the bug out, but that thing, it was hell with wings. That's what it was. Just terrifying (even if I did live to tell the tale).

takes a deep breath

How about we talk about something *way* less scary, like . . .

Fireflies

Now there is one bug I don't mind and that is a firefly. I grew up with them in the Midwest, outside of Chicago, so they really weren't anything super special to me. Not when you saw them every summer. They'd light up and it would be fun to chase them down, and you'd do fun things that you don't do as an adult, like squishing them on the sidewalk to make the pavement glow or smushing them around your finger to make a little glowy ring. (Like I said, things that I would never do as an adult. How did I become this bug fearing person? Seriously, I used to *kill* these poor fireflies to make fake jewelry! *shakes head at self*) But anyway, I grew up with fireflies and I didn't see anything special about them until I married a man from the desert state of Utah.

Joe had never seen a firefly in his life. He knew about them, of course you know about them, but he'd never seen one. Fast forward a good ten years and I'd finally convinced him to move to the East Coast. Can I just tell you how much I love this man's child-like wonder? Example: As we're driving from the desert to the East Coast, all Joe could say was, "Wow, this is so green." And every state just got greener and greener and greener. It was like he was seeing HD trees for the first time, and he couldn't believe it.

When we got there and got settled, a family invited us over to their house for dinner. They had a beautiful, big backyard with a ginormous tree in the middle of it. We sat outside most of the night, laughing, barbecuing, and enjoying the evening air. As dark descended I noticed these little bugs lighting up the darkness and felt the nostalgia of childhood wash over me.

Joe whispered to me, awed, "Oh my gosh, what is that?!" His was mesmerized.

"Those are fireflies." I glanced at him "This is what they do."

"This is the coolest thing ever!" He stood up from his chair, walked out into their backyard, and reached for these fireflies as they lit up for a moment, went dark, and then lit up again. They were leading him along this fun, fabulous, adorable journey through the backyard as he reached for their light lighting his way.

The Moral of the Stories

Now, why do I share these two stories? Because in our lives, as we travel this journey of following our Soul Songs, we will come across spider crickets and we will come across fireflies.

Spider crickets, if you go back to your first paper, are the fears and negative character traits you wrote down—they are just an illusion. Time management is an illusion. It's a skill I can learn. I know it now, I just have to implement it. Me not being worth it, that's an illusion. Of course, I'm worth it. Of course, you're worth it. Of course, that inner writer, inner being, inner soul who is begging to be free is worth it. She is beautiful, mesmerizing, and so very talented.

All those things you and I wrote down are just spider crickets that get us to jump because, for a moment, they are terrifying and we think we are facing hell with wings. And the people who show up reciting those same things to us, in that moment, they're just spider crickets too, pushing us back, moving us out of the path we know we want to travel. You can call them mental gremlins, you can call them the Adversary, you can call them Opposition, you can call it science—for every action, there's an equal and opposite reaction—you can call it whatever you want.

What it *is* is an illusion that gets us to move in a direction that we do not want to go but we go anyway because we are afraid.

On the other hand, all the positive, supportive things that we have in our lives—loving our positive traits, owning our stories, building a tribe of amazing coaches, peers and clients—those are our fireflies. They light up the darkness, remind us who we are, and encourage us to keep going on our journey. They are the ones who help us see that there is hope and goodness, there is joy and excitement, and there *is*, in fact, something better waiting on our journey if we just take one more step. They lead us into wonderment and magic rather than pushing us back into boxes and labels and fear.

Any group, event, or retreat I hold is designed to be filled with fireflies . . . fireflies wearing battle armor who are ready to take down anyone that tries to undermine the power of the people in that group. Why? Because having a powerful tribe of coaches and peers matters.

> Looking for *your* tribe? We got you! If you are a creative visionary being called to something greater in this life and you are willing share the magic that is you with the world (even if you don't know what that looks like yet) . . . come join me in Sacred Rebels: www.sacredrebels.me. It's time to live your Soul Song!

As you go about building courage . . . as you see through your fear, separate who you are from what you do, love who you are, own your story and choose your tribe over your fear, **the last thing that I want you to remember is to surround yourself with fireflies.**

The path to inner fulfillment is not always an easy one, but when we surround ourselves with the people who are ready to sing our Soul Songs when we have forgotten the words, we can borrow their courage to lead us forward on this path.

Now, I want you to go someplace where you feel comfortable making some noise. Don't worry, take your time! I'll refill my water and we'll meet back here.

races to kitchen and fills canteen

Are you in a place where you can make some noise? Wherever you are, I want you to choose courage. Take your paper—the one where you listed the thing holding you back, the fears underneath, and any negative words—and I want you to crumple it up, throw it on the floor, and STOMP the hell out of it!!!

That is what we do with a spider cricket.

We stomp, and we stomp hard, because they have *no right*, *no space*, and *no room* in our soul or on our journey to creating meaning and impact in this world. Okay?

Once you're done ripping, pushing, and stomping, you can go light this little sucker on fire or you can throw it away, whatever you need to do to get rid of it. Get it out of your space. Let it know that it no longer has power over you.

Now, I'm not saying we stomp on—bless their hearts—the friends and family who show up thinking they're helping but really are spider crickets. That's not what I'm saying.

We stomp on *the idea*, we stomp on the illusion. We control that. We can't control anyone else out there in the world—we can't stop the trolls from showing up, or the haters from sending messages—but what we can do is put that lie, that little spider cricket, where it belongs . . . Every. Single. Time.

Got it? Fabulous!

Because there is just one step left . . . and it's simultaneously the easiest and the hardest of the list.

BEHIND THE GLITTER:

Deb on Family Support

Q: What do I do if my family members are my worst critics and don't support me?

A: Allow them to just be family members and surround yourself with fireflies.

We have *so many* expectations tied up with family. They are supposed to love us unconditionally, support us just the same, be our number one cheerleaders, call us on our shit but still encourage us to the finish line of our design, while also being flawed human beings with their own thoughts, feelings, and desires about both us and themselves. Wow! That's a lot of pressure to put on people!

While some family members can fill all these roles, the truth is that many of them do not. They don't see or understand our vision and their advice to us is usually filtered through their own fears. Not to mention the box they unconsciously want to push us back into every time we try to step out. Remember how the edge of the comfort zone is death? When we try to step outside their comfort zone, their warning bells go off too and, in order to save everyone, they try to force us back into the safety zone.

Most of them don't even know they're acting as spider crickets!

So, what do we do?

We stop expecting them to be anything other than a family member (until they choose otherwise). Meaning, I don't expect my mom to cheer on my business endeavors, unless she chooses it. When we talk, I focus on "mom" type stuff. I try to ask questions about her life. I chat about things that perhaps we both are interested in. Same goes for siblings, grandparents, spouses, children, and so on. Letting go of the expectation for any of them to be my number one fan has allowed me to better enjoy our relationship and time together. And I allow the same thing for my friends.

Unless they are truly toxic. Toxic family members I limit time with. Toxic friends I remove from my ecosystem. The choice will be up to you. Listen to your intuition and don't make those choices on a bad day or based on shame. Do what's best for you.

If mental-gremlin chatter accidentally comes pouring out of the mouths of the ones we choose to keep, either exit the conversation or write and burn it later—which is simply a method of writing negative self-talk (whether yours or others) out on paper and burning it when done. You can also rip, shred, stomp, etc. Consider it "taking out the trash" when it comes to your mental, emotional, and energetic space.

> For a really phenomenal read on changing the patterns of intimate relationships, check out *The Dance of Anger* by Harriet Lerner, Ph.D. It is incredible!

Have a question? Send me your insights and comments. I want to know what you think!

https://www.debbieburns.me/contact

CHAPTER NINE:

Wash. Rinse. Repeat.

THIS LAST STEP—step seven of *The Path to Courage*—is simple and straight forward:

Keep doing the work. Daily.

When we do courage and mindset work, this is not a one and done. I did not get out of the hospital, write my 100 words, and suddenly everything was great. Wahoo! No fears and doubts ever again! The end.

That's not real, okay?

We don't find our courage once and wear it like some kind of talisman. If we are on a path to growth—which you are if you have any desire to create something in this life . . . art, books, businesses, a legacy . . . *anything*—then we are constantly stepping outside our comfort zone. We talked about that. It's the nature of growth, ever expanding into the next and the next.

Which means we're constantly encountering new fears, new failures, new mistakes, new unmet expectations. It also means we're discovering new horizons, new experiences, new people, new excitements, new joys, new adventures, new awesome, and new strengths!

The journey is incredible!!! And the way we keep moving forward and keep building courage is that we keep repeating these steps . . . every day.

So get comfortable analyzing your blocks in order to see through your fear. Stay on top of the words pouring through your mental space so you can separate who you are from what you do. Keep loving yourself, repeating those words like a sacred prayer. Keep owning your story and using it in new ways to connect with your tribe. Keep choosing those amazing, wonderful, kickass people over your fear. And keep following those fireflies—the people who see you, your potential, your Big Dream and believe just as strongly as you do that it's not just possible, it's inevitable.

Repeat.

Repeat.

Repeat.

And remember, you got this!

BEHIND THE GLITTER:

Deb on Forgiveness

Q: I have a big problem with forgiveness. Do I really have to forgive?

A: Yes.

In the recipe for change, forgiveness is the star ingredient. Change is messy and uncomfortable. Change means we are stepping into uncharted waters and doing things we have probably never done before. Change opens us up for failing, falling, and freaking out. So how do we keep from turning back and clinging to our old selves? We get really good at forgiving self . . . offering ourselves grace . . . every single time. It's the only way.

What about forgiving others?

I have a lot of clients who struggle with this. Hell! *I* used to struggle with this. Until a friend pointed out that forgiveness (a.k.a. grace) is simply a change in perspective about God, self, and/or the world.

Really? A change in perspective, huh?

As I let this sit within me, I was able to reframe forgiveness from the definition with which I was raised (forgiveness = forgetting, approving, turning the other cheek, etc.) to one that empowered me. I began to see that giving another human grace didn't mean I agreed with them, and it didn't mean that their actions or words against me were okay (because forgiveness isn't about approval). Instead, I saw that forgiveness was about letting go of what didn't serve me and shifting my perspective back toward those things that did! In this case, becoming the person I wanted to be. It was about *realignment!*

This new world view gave me permission to give their shit back to those who had hurt me and say, "This is yours. I'm not carrying it anymore."

The hate, the anger, the injustice, the shame . . . is that *really* what I wanted to keep holding in my hands? Is that what I wanted to take up space in my life? Because, I promise you, the people who hurt, abused, and otherwise mistreated me? They were getting on with their lives. Me holding onto all that junk didn't hurt them; it hurt me.

So now I choose to let it go. I hand it back. I relieve my hands of carrying that baggage so they can be open to receive *even better things* from the Universe.

And believe me, I haven't forgotten. Not even in the slightest. But I can remember without hurting. That, to me, is progress.

When I forgive (or ask for forgiveness!), whatever the other person does or doesn't do afterward is their problem. They don't have to accept it and they don't have to apologize in return. I have done my work to return to alignment.

I am free to move forward.

Have a question? Send me your insights and comments. I want to know what you think!
https://www.debbieburns.me/contact

CHAPTER TEN:

Two Roads Diverged

Two roads diverged in a wood, and I—
I took the one less traveled by,
And that has made all the difference.

~Robert Frost, *The Road Not Taken*

A Day in Your Life if *Nothing* Were to Change

PICTURE THIS . . . A DAY in your life one year from now.

365 days ago, you read this strange book called *The Path to Courage*. It was everything you'd been searching for! Almost as if the Universe had placed it into your path in answer to the call you'd put out for something different, something better, something more. It lit your soul on fire! And, for that brief moment, you saw everything your future could be!!!! But then you closed the cover, put it on your shelf, and went back to living your practical life.

"It's for everyone else," you thought, "not for me."

So here you are now, living the same-old-same-old life. You keep doing things "their way" expecting a different result. You keep trying to make yourself fit, blend in, be a part of whatever it is that's happening around you. You're not miserable, but you're not happy. But you can live with that, right? Maybe you just aren't meant to be extremely happy. It's not for everyone. You can find happiness in the mundane, can't you?

You march to the beat of someone else's drum, working the job, paying the bills, buying the house, the car, the 2.5 kids. It's all nice. And it is! It's nice. But it's not . . . *filling*.

You wish you had more time with your partner, but you both are busy trying to make it all work, passing each other during the rush hours of the house.

"Can you pick up the milk?"

"Yeah, make sure you get the towels in the dryer."

When was the last time you really talked? You shrug, not able to remember. But hey, this is just how life goes.

It's just . . .

　　how life . . .

　　　　goes.

And as you get into bed for the night, you accidentally kick a dust-covered book peeking out from beneath the bed: *The Path to Courage*. You sit on the edge of your mattress, gingerly touching the title, and you wonder, "What if? What if I'd said yes one year ago?"

A Day in Your Life if You Follow Your Soul Song

Imagine this . . .

365 days ago, you read this interesting book called *The Path to Courage*. It was everything you'd been searching for! Almost as if the Universe had placed it into your path in answer to the call you'd put out for something different, something better, something more. It lit your soul on fire! And, for that brief moment, you saw everything your future could be!!!!

Your soul sang, your Higher Self shouted HELL YES!!! And you—in spite of your fear, past failures and current mental-gremlin obstacles—went running straight into the arms of your awaiting greatness!

"Why not me?" you thought, "Why can't I listen to my Soul Song, follow my Big Dream, and live my Happily EPIC After?!!!"

And so now, here you are! Living a life that has surpassed all your wildest dreams!!! You open your email to see another request to participate in someone else's podcast. They love your work and want to share it with their tribe! You do a quick check of your calendar—live interview here, holding your workshop/retreat/event there, travel to Spain two weeks later—Yep! You can totally fit this interview into your schedule! And your new book perfectly aligns with this podcaster's needs!!! You feel the warmth spread from your heart—pure joy—at being able to serve at this expansive level.

You are doing things *your* way, dancing to the rhythm of your Big Dream. Contrary to your fears a year ago, you see yourself surrounded by people who truly care and support you—real belonging, with you invested in them and they in you. You check Voxer and send off a quick note of appreciation to one of your Fireflies who helped you through a recent obstacle.

You smile remembering how at one time you thought you had to create a life without fear in order to feel successful. But *this*, this feels so good knowing that fear and obstacles aren't a sign that you're broken or doing it wrong. They're simply an indicator that you are still on your path of growth and expansion.

"Bring it on!" you say out loud. Your partner laughs and gives you a big hug, so proud of you. So very proud. You feel more connected to your partner than ever. Sure, there are hard conversations to be had, you're both human. But you love that you are having them. You are talking and connecting. You are creating a powerful life together.

"I have a few hours," you tell your partner. "Want to get breakfast?!"

"Yes!"

Bills are getting paid, dreams are being fulfilled, lives are being changed . . . all because you said HELL YES to you.

And as you get into bed for the night—after a day filled with awesome client calls, appreciation emails, time with your loved ones, handling a tough conversation in complete alignment with you, fulfilling work, and new insights—you accidentally kick a well-used book peeking out from beneath the bed. You laugh, picking up *The Path to Courage* as you sit on the edge of your mattress, lovingly touching the cover. "I wonder what's next . . ."

You smile as you place it back on the nightstand. Because you know that living your Happily EPIC After means tomorrow will be filled with surprises.

> If your soul is singing HELL YES to your own Happily EPIC after and you want a guide to help you move forward, you know what to do: www.sacredrebels.me.

BEHIND THE GLITTER:

Deb on Money

Q: I can't commit to investing in me or my Big Dream right now. I only make X and I have to pay Y and Z. (I know it sounds like a story. It's just a reality.) What do I do?

A: You're right; it *does* sound like a story.

While there are a few cases where people just don't have the money to invest in themselves and their Big Dream (believe you me . . . part of my childhood was spent in government housing where roaches scattered when you turned on the light), more often than not it's a matter of priorities.

We *have* the money to spend, but *where* are we choosing to spend it?

There is no judgement here. You are allowed to invest your dollars wherever you desire. This is about being *aware* of why you are choosing to put your funds toward one thing over another. (Instead of choosing into the belief that you don't have any.)

It's about *seeing through* the fear.

Remember that "what's holding you back?" question from chapter three? Money is just another excuse for not choosing into our Big Dream. What you really want to be asking yourself is, "What's underneath my I-don't-have-money story? What is the deeper fear? What is really holding me back?"

Because, I promise, there is definitely something deeper going on when our soul says HELL YES to our next step but we choose out (almost automatically) with "I don't have the money for that." And until we know what that deeper issue is, we will continue to choose everything else over our Big Dream.

I know because I was there, promising myself someday while letting everything but what I wanted most take center stage.

"Next time, Deb," I'd tell myself. "Next time." But

next time never came. Until, face down on the rough, Berber carpet, I thought I would die.

Friend, there is *never* a good time to invest in your dreams. There will always be more reasons to choose out than reasons to choose in, and more reasons to invest in everyone and everything but ourselves. The longer we wait, the harder it is to choose now over someday.

So ask yourself, "What is it costing me in time, energy, joy, fulfillment, and money to stand in fear rather than courage? What is it costing me to DIY a solution instead of getting expert advice? **What will it cost me in regret if my life were to stay exactly the same?**"

And, when you're ready to step forward, ask yourself, "Who can help me?" Because there are people out there who will answer the call and be your miracle.

When I was looking to make the *biggest* investment of my life in me and my biz ($20,000), I knew I didn't have it. And I knew I couldn't afford the payments this coach offered. But my soul was singing HELL YES so loud my husband could hear it. So we asked this question, "Who can help me?" We listened and wrote down the list of names. We called every single one and got rejection after rejection. And on the last call (SOOO hard because these were successful friends of ours and we didn't want to make things "weird"), they said yes and became our miracle.

If you honest-to-grandma can't afford a program, mentor, coach or course, become *hella good* at taking what is offered for free and *putting it into action.* Otherwise, you have to evaluate your priorities and get your fear out of the way.

If you're struggling with money or have money-related questions, go to: www.josephmburns.com. He's the Money Master helping peeps re-write their personal money playbook.

Have a question? Send me your insights and comments. I want to know what you think!
https://www.debbieburns.me/contact

CHAPTER ELEVEN:

Next Steps

SQUEE!!!! I HOPE YOU choose the rabbit hole, my friend! (That's what I call doing the thing that takes you on an alternate path from your current trajectory.) I hope you follow your Soul Song and live your Happily EPIC After!!!! I hope you'll take the first few steps today that will get you to that bright, brilliant, beautiful future waiting for you tomorrow.

So, pulling it all together in one nice little bundle, here's what to do to put yourself on the path to courage:

1. **Write down what's getting in the way of your Big Dream** and ask yourself, "Why?" Look for the fear that is hiding beneath the excuse.

2. **Create your 100-word list** of positive qualities and characteristics that make up who you are. (Remember, you can get my free PDF

download here: www.pathtocourage.com/100 words.)

3. **Post your 100-word list everywhere** and, using the phrase, "I love that I am _____," say your words out loud, daily.

4. **Own your story by sharing it** with someone outside yourself!

5. **Pick one thing that you have been hesitating to do because of fear and *do* that thing.** (Don't forget to tell me about it: hello@debbie burns.me!)

6. **Take your paper from step 1 and crumple it up, throw it on the floor, and stomp the hell out of it!!!** Then burn it for good measure! (Be safe and burn it outside in a controlled area. If you burn your house down, it's not my fault.)

7. **Repeat.** Use your tools daily to make your way through fear, failure, and mental-gremlins so you can follow your Soul Song and live your Happily EPIC After!

That's it! You got this!

BEHIND THE GLITTER:

Deb on Resistance

Q: I keep getting resistance as I lean into my Big Dream. Is that a sign I should stop?

A: Nope. It's a sign to pause.

Resistance is a natural part of growth. Think about going to the gym to sculpt a lean body. Do you show up, ready to do nothing? "Sorry trainer-dude, the second I lifted that weight, I felt resistance, which means I should stop." Nah, we wouldn't *do* that because we've been trained to work hard at the gym. We lift the weights, we run on the treadmill, we do whatever it takes to sweat!

And yet, when we want to create strong dream-building muscles as we grow into our Happily EPIC After, suddenly we think that resistance equals failure, a bad choice, or missed inspiration.

When, really, it's just energetic weight added to the reps we're doing so we can strengthen our courage and develop our Soul Song!

So why pause? Why not just barrel straight ahead? Because we need to be *aware*. Going back to my gym analogy, if I'm not listening to my body when it feels resistance, I can give myself *too much* weight, harming my muscle and doing serious damage.

Likewise, we want to pay attention to the energetic resistance. Am I giving myself too much to handle at once? Am I balancing my energy outgo with things that fill me back in? Am I listening to the nuances of my intuition so I know when to speed up, when to slow down, and when to take a break?

If you are feeling the resistance as you lean into your Soul Song, CONGRATULATIONS! You are on your way to building a dream that will give you the joy and fulfillment you desire.

(Just don't do that thing where you work so hard on your first day at the gym that you puke on the guy next to you and never come back, okay?

Wait . . . that hasn't happened to you? Yeah . . . me either.)

Have a question? Send me your insights and comments. I want to know what you think!
https://www.debbieburns.me/contact

CONCLUSION:

Piece of My Heart

FIRES GLITTER CANNONS

That. Was. INCREDIBLE!!!!!

I have *loved* starting this journey with you and sharing all my heartbeats and insights. Thank you, thank you, thank you for being an active participant on *your Path to Courage*. Thank you for being open to the process. Thank you for trying something new, something weird, something different. Thank you for sharing your work with the world and for empowering others by showing up for you.

It's hard to leave you here when there is still so much awesome to create together! So much for you to know about your Soul Song and so much light to shine on the dark places of your fear.

I want you to know that on this journey there will be days when you just feel like you can't take one more step. There will be times when you ask yourself, "Oh gosh, what am I doing and why did

I pick this?!" And, "There's got to be an easier way . . . why can't people just support me?" There are going to be moments when you want to take what you're doing and shut it down because you feel like, "Maybe I'm not meant to do this big thing after all."

Please hear me when I say this . . . those are mental gremlin lies!

If you need to take a pause, take a pause, but please don't give up. Please don't let go of your dream. Please don't stop following your Soul Song. That song came to you for a reason and this world needs it. Please lean in and, if you need a tribe of battle ready fireflies, come join me.

Repeat your tools daily. Find your fireflies. Take your action. Own your story. Practice loving who you are. Separate who you are from what you do. And please, please, please, please, please, please, see through your fears and run *toward* your greatness.

Dear Sacred Rebel, I love you, I love you, I love you. You belong. May my heartbeats give you courage until you can trust your own.

And remember . . .

> You *are* the one, the right one, the beautifully imperfect one who has been called to change the world.

I believe in you, my friend. All that is left is for you to believe in you too.

SOUL PACT:

Sacred Rebels Answer the Call

To live outside the box.
To smash the locks and break the gates
holding us back from our truest potential—
as defined by self, not someone else.

To journey.
To discover.
To create.

To claim our freedom, our hope,
our authentic self.
To taste life and experience new horizons.
To live our passions and impact the world
as only we can.

This is why we breathe.
And we are too powerful to play it small.

ACKNOWLEDGMENTS

Oh gosh! This is where my little heart explodes in glitter! Both for the joy and gratitude for those who have helped me on my own path to courage, and with anxiety because "what if I get this wrong?! Or leave someone out?!" Aaaahhhhh!!!!!

breathes into brown paper bag

Well, here it goes. Taking my own medicine to feel the fear, puke glitter, and do it anyway!!!

All My Heartbeats Go To:

My life and business partner, Joe Burns, for always encouraging me toward my greatness, and for hearing my Soul Song and singing it back to me when I have forgotten the words. Thank you for believing in my Big Dream, for trusting me with our future, for choosing me when we first got married and for choosing me again when we almost got divorced. It's been one hell of a ride, and I am so incredibly happy I get to experience this adventure with you!!!! To our Happily EPIC After!!!

My business coach, Jennifer Kem, for seeing potential in me that I didn't see or believe in myself.

You've nurtured me every step of the way, pushed me when you knew I needed to play bigger, comforted me when you knew I needed rest, encouraged me when you knew it was time to transition, and held my feet to the fire when you knew *this* was the time to go all in and *not* back down. Thank you. I love you.

My book mentor, Kathy Kidd. Oh sweet sassy molassey!!! You've been telling me for at least the last year (if not longer!) that I could write this book. That I *needed* to write it. And you've walked me through the process, holding my hand, calming my fears, and reminding me of my own truths. Thank you for shining your light for so many authors and providing the way for us to succeed!!!

My book team—Chelsea Fitch, Daniela Freeman, Dorothy Tinker, and Taylor Birch—for all your artistic, marketing, editing, and technical support and for making this as beautiful outside as I believe it is on the inside. And my photographer, Meagan Smith!!! Damn, girl! You made me look good!

My Glitter Posse!!! All the super tackle squishy hugs ever to: Sarah Paikai, Denise Kelly, Chelsea Fitch, Lynne Maureen Hurdle, Lindsay Paikai, Hillary Weiss, Birdy Jones, Laura Moss, Maria Volovik,

Rachel Anzalone, and Meagan Alder. Thank you for seeing me, loving me, encouraging me, and giving me the real tough love when you knew I needed it!!! You ladies inspire me to reach for better words and greater courage every day of my life. Thank you for reminding me that I *can* and I *will* and I *am*. I love, love, love you. Always and forever.

My miracles, Chelsie and Ryan Lawson, without whom these past two years wouldn't have been possible. Thank you for believing in me and this work I do. I love you guys!

My brother, Jason Smith, for being the first to teach me that I should always be myself. It took me awhile to figure out who that was! But your encouragement to be true to me got me through some of the most difficult parts.

YOU—the beautiful, amazing visionary and sacred rebel who is looking for a way to choose your Soul Song—including your message, tribe, passion and impact—over your fear. I believe in you!

And, finally, a deep, deep thank you to the women who once held space for my own healing among sterile white walls and whimpers in the night. Seeing your courage emboldened my own. I will never forget you.

ABOUT THE AUTHOR

Debbie Burns (a.k.a. Deb and Debbers) loves to travel, write, make people laugh, and explore all facets of life (inner and outer) as she spreads glitter, champions love, and encourages people to believe in their own brand of magic. She dreams of being on The Ellen DeGeneres Show (who doesn't?!) and *finally* developing the courage to scuba dive—in a pool. (Baby steps, friend. Open water is *the shark's* house!)

Deb has attended writing, business, and marketing conferences all over the states, has seen the rise (and decline) of Twitter, loves Netflix and binge reading, and speaks on stages nationwide. She is an international bestselling author and founder of Fiction Expedition (for lady fiction writers), Sacred Rebels, and many other delicious programs and transformative experiences.

You can find her clickety-clacking away in Utah (though she's always on the lookout for her next big adventure!) as she lives her Happily EPIC After with her husband Joe and her not-so-little-but-totally-adorable pittie, Josser.

www.ingramcontent.com/pod-product-compliance
Lightning Source LLC
La Vergne TN
LVHW051643080426
835511LV00016B/2465